Railway Moods

THE EAST LANCASHIRE RAILWAY

MIKE HEATH

HALSGROVE

First published in Great Britain in 2006

British Library Cataloguing-in-Publication Data
A CIP record for this title is available from the British Library

ISBN 1 84114 524 6
ISBN 978 1 84114 524 2

HALSGROVE
Halsgrove House
Lower Moor Way
Tiverton, Devon EX16 6SS
Tel: 01884 243242
Fax: 01884 243325
email: sales@halsgrove.com
website: www.halsgrove.com

Printed and bound by D'Auria Industrie Grafiche Spa, Italy

Bury Bolton Street Station dates from 1846, was rebuilt and enlarged during the 1880s and in its heyday witnessed over 100 departures a day. It is now home to the East Lancashire Railway Preservation Society which took control following the cessation of electric train services to Manchester in 1980. The train in platform 3 is the next departure to Rawtenstall.

The entrance to the station, which was rebuilt in the 1950s following a fire, is at road level with access to the platforms via staircases leading down from the footbridge seen in this view from platform 2.

An historic day for the Society was 27 April 1991, which saw the first passenger train run through to Rawtenstall. Of particular interest is the leading locomotive which was built in 1903, by Hudswell-Clarke, for the Manchester Ship Canal Company.

The railway is also home to a substantial diesel fleet which sees regular use alternating with steam services on certain days.

Once a year the role of the railways in wartime is commemorated with a weekend of events. The wearing of period clothing is actively encouraged.

Set pieces for night-time photography are also a feature of some special event weekends.

Here the camera has moved closer as if to eavesdrop on the railwaymen's conversation.

With steam hissing from every valve a train eases away on a crisp winter's day.

Opposite: The floodlighting set up on photography evenings can provide pleasing results. However, whenever possible I prefer to use available station lighting. All night running allows scenes such as this to be captured. The covering of snow reflects available light onto the locomotive's wheels.

13

On leaving Bury the train almost immediately passes through the 80-yards-long Bury EL Tunnel which runs beneath Bolton Street. It emerges alongside the former East Lancashire Railway's warehouse and goods yard at Castlecroft.

In 1972 the Preservation Society found a new home at Castlecroft, relocated its locos and rolling stock there, and created the Bury Transport Museum. Two years later two tank engines were acquired from the Manchester Ship Canal Company and, with a section of track having been cleared, they were able to offer brake van rides to visitors. Pictured here is locomotive No. 70 'Phoenix'. The other was No. 32 'Gothenburg' referred to on page 7.

A three road shed was built between the yard and the 'main line' and provided many photographic opportunities during the early hours of a summer's day…

...and on a cold winter's morning.

Even without the floodlights, the backlighting from the shed created a very atmospheric scene.

Opposite: It was also an excellent location for night photography under specially positioned floodlighting.

However, the main purpose of the shed was to provide shelter and maintenance facilities for the locomotive fleet, which it did until the former Electric Locomotive shed at Buckley Wells became available in 1993.

Shortly after leaving Bury the valley becomes rural and the first of nine crossings over the River Irwell is made.

A change of season and the abundant vegetation has closed in to form a natural frame.

Opposite: With the line running north-south at this location, a low winter's afternoon sun affords the opportunity to capture the train in silhouette as it crosses the bridge.

Equally, with the low afternoon sun behind the camera the whole side of the locomotive is highlighted.

At this point the railway passes the former settlement of Burrs and is the most popular photographic location on the railway, as the line climbs on a shallow embankment making the locomotives work hard. Here, during a winter gala, an early morning demonstration freight train is forging its way north.

Again, with the sun setting against a clear blue sky, another dramatic silhouette is captured.

(Photo. Karl Heath)

It is not always necessary for the train to be visible in the photograph. (This is the first of a number of photographs in the book taken by my younger son Karl. I fear he's becoming too good at this hobby!)

This is a 'typical' Burrs photograph where the footplate crew are putting on a show for the assembled gallery of photographers.

In August 1993 the railway held a Festival of Steam to commemorate the end of steam on British Rail and twenty-five years of the Society. A variety of locomotives from other preservation sites were invited to attend including this peculiar locomotive built by Sentinel Ltd (famous for steam wagons) in 1933. It worked at the London and North Eastern Railway's permanent way works at Darlington. For the technically minded it has a water tube boiler and vertical cylinders inside the cab. The crankshaft is totally enclosed and runs in an oil bath. The drive to the four wheels is by two roller chains. It is no record-breaker and normally resides at the Middleton Railway Centre, Leeds.

Another morning scene from August 1991 as the 9am double-headed departure from Bury passes by.

The area around Burrs has been developed as a country park which from a railway photographer's point of view is unfortunate as the land in the foreground is to become a caravan park rendering this, and the next, photograph un-repeatable.

There is also a long term plan for a halt at this location to serve the country park. However, this is just another period of evolution for the railway and its surroundings which, as in the past, will create different photographic opportunities.

Between Burrs and the first station at Summerseat the railway passes through a cutting before the valley narrows as the river cuts into its sides, with the line passing through wooded cloughs following the lazy curves of the river.

The locomotive seen here bathed in winter sunshine with steam condensing in the cold air, is over 100 years old. No. 1300 was built at Horwich in 1896 for the Lancashire and Yorkshire Railway and, as it spent much of its working life based at Newton Heath shed in Manchester, it was no doubt a regular visitor to this line in its previous life.

Opposite: In the winter months the natural frame formed by the bare branches of trees can produce very attractive results. Add some low afternoon sunlight glinting off a hard-working locomotive, and a spectacular scene can result.

As the train enters the cutting on the approach to Summerseat it crosses the main footpath along the valley. The locations for the photographs on pages 33 and 34 are reached by following the path seen climbing away on the opposite side of the track.

This photograph is a little deceptive as the diesel is actually at the rear of a Santa Special train that is about to pass through Summerseat Station at the far end of the cutting. Diesels are employed on these services to haul the return journeys thus saving the time that would be necessary if the steam locomotive had to run round the train at Ramsbottom.

One of the most dramatic photographs I have taken on a railway. An early morning double-headed departure from Summerseat on Boxing Day 1992

Opposite: At Summerseat only one of the original platforms remains. What was left of the other has been used to help the extension of the platform at Ramsbottom. Up until the line's closure in 1972 there had been no bus service to the village, and even now the railway is the only provider of public transport to the area on Sundays!

Just beyond the station is arguably the most attractive location on the railway. This impressive structure is the 200-yards-long Brooksbottom Viaduct. Behind the viaduct are the buildings of a former dye works and cotton mill which have been converted to luxury flats and a bar restaurant. From late morning onwards the sun, when it appears, bathes this side of the line with light, making this the popular view.

The last light of the day emphasises the locomotive's exhaust against a crystal-clear blue sky.

Early risers have the opportunity to capture the opposite view. Unique locomotive No. 71000 'Duke of Gloucester' is a regular visitor to the line. Built as a one-off, it entered service in 1954, but due to dieselisation of the West Coast main line it never really operated to its full potential being withdrawn in 1962 with only 300,000 miles on the clock. It made its first run in preservation in1986 and since 1990 has hauled many main line specials. Its performances are noted as being far better than any in the days of British Rail!

(Photo. Karl Heath)

From Holcombe Hill on a clear day the panoramic views are spectacular and you can follow the progress of the train for virtually the whole journey along the valley. The plume of steam in the centre of the photograph draws attention to the train as it crosses the viaduct.

Immediately after crossing the viaduct the line enters Brooksbottom Tunnel. To the left is a cobbled track that winds its way uphill. This is Starling Street, a local mill track that stretches to Ramsbottom and which, for many years, has provided some excellent locations from where to photograph the trains. Here a winter's grip is clearly evident in this frosty landscape.

Taken from almost the same spot on a much warmer day and many years earlier. In fact this photograph dates from 1989 when the railway had only just re-opened to Ramsbottom. In those days the railway relied on humble industrial tank engines to haul most of its services. This northern section of the Irwell Valley is famous for its association with Sir Robert Peel, the Prime Minister who hailed from Bury, and the railway maintained this link by conferring his name on this locomotive in 1988.

Once through Brooksbottom Tunnel the railway passes along a short narrow cutting before entering a second, the 115-yards-long Nuttall Tunnel. This photographer's chartered demonstration freight train is emerging from Nuttall Tunnel on a very damp and miserable day when conditions made photography very difficult.

Opposite: To the left a train is approaching the mouth of the tunnel. Starling Street climbs above to the right.

Between the tunnels and Ramsbottom Station the gradient of the line levels out to 1 in 264 and the valley widens out as the river forms a great meander. January 1991 and a post-Christmas Gala Special climbs away from the tunnel.

Opposite: The equivalent weekend five years later, and the weather has provided a Christmas-card landscape for the event.

For this photograph I was standing on the edge of Ramsbottom's vast Nuttall Park. The two previous photographs were taken from the field behind the tree beyond the locomotive.

Crossing the same bridge in February 1993 is the world's most famous locomotive 'Flying Scotsman' which was visiting as part of a tour of preserved railways.

An interesting combination on the final approach to the station. The leading engine, built in 1896, and last seen in its original livery on page 34, had previously been painted in British Rail colours and in this earlier view is paired with a representative of the last class of locomotive built by BR, class 9F No. 92203, which dates from 1959.

At Ramsbottom all that was left by British Railways was a single bare platform. The station has therefore had to be almost totally rebuilt and the main building was constructed in the original East Lancashire Railway style that had been adopted for smaller stations on the original line. It was completed in 1989. With Santa Special trains terminating at Ramsbottom the railway operates a shuttle service between here and Rawtenstall, which on this particular day was in the hands of a two car diesel multiple unit.

Following plans of an original Lancashire and Yorkshire Railway design the society scratch built the water tower.

Opposite: The railway operates regular evening dining trains on selected Fridays during the year. These give passengers the opportunity to enjoy a luxury evening meal served aboard a train hauled by a vintage steam locomotive. In this scene, captured at dusk, guests on the 'Red Rose Diner' are stretching their legs between courses.

The signal box, signals, footbridge and level crossing all combine to create a 1950's appearance, particularly under the station lights at night.

The Winter Steam Galas at the end of January have the added attraction of trains running into the night. At the 2001 event I spent the evening photographing trains as they paused alongside the platforms.

The power of the steam forcing its way through the safety valves, and the light of the locomotive fires illuminating the footplates has created this evocative time exposure photograph.

Despite the anti-photography weather on a damp January evening in 1993 I visited Ramsbottom to photograph 'Flying Scotsman' at the head of that evening's Dining Train. Imagine my surprise and delight when through the mist at the far end of the platform came the sound, followed by the sight, of these two Scottish Pipers marching towards me. A photographer should never be put off by bad weather!

There was an icy blast in the air as the New Year dawned in 1997 and with the snow on the ground accompanied by bright sunshine the photographic possibilities could not be resisted. Here strong backlighting has given a silhouette appearance to the locomotive and its crew as the water tanks are refilled.

Opposite: The cold is almost tangible in this photograph. Believe me the duo warming their hands on the brazier became a trio as soon as soon as the shutter had closed.

Judging by the icicles hanging from the water tank, the brazier certainly had its work cut out on this occasion!

Time for the off and the signalman offers the token, for the Rawtenstall section, to the crew of the elegantly streamlined London and North Eastern Railway A4 class locomotive No 4498 which carries the name of the class designer ' Sir Nigel Gresley'.

In the latter years of British Rail's operations the signalbox existed merely to operate the level crossing. It has now been re-quipped to a very high standard and controls all movements through, in and around the station.

(Photo. Karl Heath)

Ramsbottom, the crossing point for the line to Rawtenstall where footplate crews will have exchanged tokens, through the signalman, before continuing their journey, is primarily a victorian town that grew from the small settlement that existed when Robert Peel Senior opened a calico printing works in 1783. Development as a textile town continued through the nineteenth century with mills for spinning, weaving and of course printing appearing in the landscape. In this second autumnal view from Holcombe Hill the north-bound train is on its way to Rawtenstall (centre).

Above Ramsbottom the countryside becomes more attractive with wooded areas affording fine views for passengers and ramblers alike. At Stubbins the original main line to Accrington diverged and began to climb the valley side. Just north of the junction both lines had to cross the River Irwell and this photograph was taken from beneath the higher Alderbottom Viaduct which use to carry the line to Accrington.

Opposite: Irwell Vale on a wonderfully clear winter's day. The route of the former Accrington line can be clearly determined in the middle distance.

Pre-preservation there was only a mill siding at this location. However, it was decided that the restored railway should provide a service for the village and its neighbouring newly-built-up area. This was done in preference to re-opening the former Ewood Bridge and Edenfield Station located a little further up the line.

Lancashire County Council undertook building the station which, although completed in 1989 had to wait until the re-opening to Rawtenstall to witness the sights and sounds of steam. Visiting in 1992, Battle of Britain class 4-6-2 No. 34072 '257 Squadron' huffs and puffs away from the platform.

On the night of 24 February 2001 my younger son Karl and I travelled to Rawtenstall for some night photography of that evening's trains. Whilst there we were forced to take shelter from a tremendous snowstorm. With freezing temperatures forecast for overnight we realised that the lying snow was unlikely to have thawed by morning. Returning next day in superb conditions we were able to take a number of photographs capturing the much sought after sun, snow and steam at the northern end of the line.

The village which can be seen in the background owes its existence to the Irwell Vale Cotton Mill and actually pre-dates the railway. The settlement is on the west bank of the River Irwell where it is joined by a second river, the Ogden. Another photograph taken during 'Flying Scotsman's' visit in 1993.

An embankment carries the railway away from Irwell Vale past a water meadow before it again crosses the river on the first of two newly-constructed bridges, replacements for the original structures. The bill for the two bridges totalled £330,000 and they are designed to last for 100 years. I must make a note in my diary!

Opposite: A closer look at the first new bridge and a second view of A4 'Sir Nigel Gresley'. When this locomotive first visited the line it was running in the LNER blue livery as seen in the photograph on page 64. By 1995 it had been repainted into British Railway lined blue livery as No. 60007.

The second new bridge is a spot which will long remain in my memory. I identified it many years ago as a location where, given the right conditions, I would be able to get a good reflection shot. Believe me it took many visits and no few wellies full of water before all required conditions were met.

Opposite: Still, I am sure you will agree that those many days of cursing and soggy socks were all worthwhile with eventual results like these.

These next two photographs, taken from the other side of the bridge, provide links with my previous books. Former London Midland and Scottish locomotive No.5690 'Leander' featured in the award-winning photograph included in my album on the Severn Valley Railway.

Former Great Western Railway locomotive No.7822 'Foxcote Manor' visited, from the Llangollen Railway in Wales, during June 2003 and featured in my book on that line.

The railway may be relatively new in preservation terms but has attracted a vast array of different locomotives to operate on the line. In 1997 the National Railway Museum's former London Midland and Scottish Railway Coronation class 4-6-2 No. 46229 'Duchess of Hamilton' visited.

Opposite: Once the bridges have been crossed the line climbs towards an over-bridge which carries the original Bury to Haslingden turnpike road. This is another favourite viewpoint for photographers to capture locomotives hard at work against the gradient, particularly in early morning sunlight.

At this point the river has temporarily turned away and the railway runs alongside the full length of the local football team's pitch. I often wonder how many goals have been scored as attention is drawn by a passing train!

But that would not have a problem on this particular weekend when all activities would have been confined to the warmth of the new clubhouse.

(Photo. Karl Heath)

Beyond Ewood Bridge the valley begins to narrow again and the gradient increases to 1 in 150 as the 'modern' by-pass linking Haslingden and Rawtenstall with the M66 motorway is approached. With the sun, just out of shot to the right, providing soft backlighting, a nice glint has highlighted the locomotive details.

Opposite: This photograph was taken beneath the road bridge from what was once the 'up' (towards London) platform and now is all that remains of Ewood Bridge and Edenfield Station.

On a crisp winter's morning the train has passed beneath the by-pass and is about to be reunited with the river. Helmshore, the village on the hillside, once had woollen and cotton mills; nowadays they are put to other uses, however, and following the efforts of the Local History Society, one has re-opened as a working museum.

A walk along the riverside path, from Ewood Bridge, provided the opportunity to watch 'Flying Scotsman' recreate a scene once commonplace on the east coast main line between London's Kings Cross and Edinburgh's Waverley stations.

A rock cutting leads towards Rawtenstall West signal box which is a British Rail style box controlling a level crossing and all locomotive movements in and out of the terminus.

(Photo. Karl Heath)

Rawtenstall, the railway's terminus, is at the heart of Rossendale where a vista of grand mills and huge chapels is a reminder of this once prosperous cotton town's history. There was nothing more than a derelict platform here when the Society took over but, like Ramsbottom, it has received a new building in an original style, together with a clock tower similar to one which once stood at Bury's Bolton Street Station.

A night-time arrival illuminated by the platform lights. In-keeping with the Society's ability to make use of derelict buildings discarded by British Railways the shelter seen here came from Walkden Station.

Watching me, watching you. Little did I realise it at the time, but it appears that my wintry night-time photographic exploits were being filmed. Perhaps the hope was that I would slip on the snow and perform a 'triple toe loop' providing the video cameraman with a submission to 'You've been framed'!

This was the night of the sudden snowfall referred to earlier. The locomotive has run round the train and is about to commence the return journey to Bury.

Like that at Ramsbottom, the water tower was built by the Society based on original Lancashire and Yorkshire Railway drawings. An early morning freight train is pulling out of the station.

The railway's ability to recreate scenes from the past is beyond question. What is notable in this picture is the now dated method of hay baling in the adjacent field. No shrink wrapped balls of hay to be seen here!

Opposite: I have always liked the 'blood and custard' livery carried by some of British Railways' coaching fleet in the 1950s. It is especially photogenic in a rich landscape with a clear blue sky as here where a scattering of Buttercups adds colour to the foreground. The train is skirting the river as it retraces its steps down the valley.

Ancient and modern forms of transport side by side on a lovely summer's morning. The locomotive's crimson livery stands out in in the green landscape.

As shadows lengthen on lovely winter's afternoon the train has passed beneath the by-pass and is nearing Ewood Bridge. This view was taken from Blackburn Road on the opposite side of the valley.

Not the most interesting background, but in the foreground is one of the two 'new' bridges that had to be constructed. Note the detail of the new concrete bridge deck supported by the original stone piers.

I would like to say that there was a lot of pre-planning in the preparation of this carefully composed picture but it was actually a case of right place, right time. Having parked my car in the only available space at Irwell Vale, I looked left and immediately noted the natural framing for the scene. Fortunately the next southbound train was being hauled by a Bury-facing locomotive and, with storm clouds gathering above the valley, the sun stayed out just long enough to light the photograph. A few months later the leaves of the trees would have obliterated virtually all the sky and the centre section of the train!

Passing the same location in 2001 is another locomotive loaned from the National Railway Museum in York. Former London and North Eastern Railway Class V2 No. 60800 'Green Arrow' is one of a fleet of locomotives restored to main-line standard and has hauled specials all over the country.

A blanket of undisturbed snow covered the valley above Ramsbottom on the morning of 25 February 2001. By lunchtime it had all but thawed with many photographers down the line at Bury totally unaware that it had ever existed.

Reflecting the growing interest in more modern heritage traction the railway holds regular Diesel Galas throughout the year. This Bury-bound train is passing over the level crossing at the north end of Ramsbotom Station.

LMS No. 5407, one of Sir William Stanier-designed Class 5 Mixed Traffic 4-6-0 locomotives, better known as 'Black Fives', has itself had an interesting history. Built in 1937 it actually lasted right up to the end of steam on British Rail in 1968, finishing its former working life allocated to Lostock Hall shed near Preston. Since then restoration at Carnforth was followed by a number of main line special duties in the 1970s and whilst it is now a familiar sight on the ELR it continues to perform main line duties in England, Wales and Scotland and must be one of the busiest of the restored steam locomotive fleet.

Another main line performer, three years older and some distance from its former stomping ground, is Great Western Railway 4-6-0 Castle Class locomotive No. 7029 'Clun Castle'. These elegant machines used to ply their trade between London, the West Country and Wales, with Birkenhead being the most northerly destination.

Normally based at Tyseley Locomotive Works, Birmingham, it visited the line in 1994 and was photographed at the head of an afternoon freight awaiting the right-away from Ramsbottom.

Also awaiting permission to return to Bury is this evening passenger working. Notice how the wet surface emphasises the pattern of the platform's natural stone paving.

Opposite: Dusk on an autumn evening with the last vestiges of colour in the sky providing a splendid backdrop to this timeless scene.

On an evening many years earlier a mist is descending in the distance and red hot coals drop from the locomotive's ashpan as it waits patiently alongside the platform.

Another example of night photography using available light from the platform lamps producing superb results. Taken from the southern tip of the platform, the time exposure has highlighted the wisps of steam hissing from the locomotive safety valves and the carriages' steam heating pipes, and has even picked out the stars pinpricking through the deep-blue night sky.

With the signal aloft a 'traditional' railway photograph depicts a spirited departure for Bury. The pure white exhaust contrasts sharply with the storm clouds gathering above the valley.

On a bright winter's day it's the blanket of snow that provides the contrast.

Representatives of all the 'big four' pre-nationalisation companies have visited the railway at one time or another. Crossing the Irwell just south of Ramsbottom is former Southern Railway 4-6-2 Merchant Navy Class No. 35005 'Canadian Pacific'. This class was originally built in the forties with air smoothed casing, similar to that on '257 Squadron' pictured on page 69. During the following decade they were rebuilt to the more conventional appearance seen here.

As mentioned earlier, only one of the original platforms remains at Summerseat. However, in place of the other is a beautifully maintained garden which provides a colourful border all year round – the result of much hard work by a small band of enthusiastic volunteers.

A photograph only really possible in winter when the sunlight can break through the bare trees. Taken from the footpath crossing just south of Summerseat, Bury-facing 'Green Arrow' sprints past.

Opposite: The absence of turning facilities on many preserved railways means that tender-first running is unavoidable. One of the footplate crew basks in the sunshine on the steam locomotive's 'crows nest' checking that the road ahead is clear.

Another photograph taken from a footpath crossing, this time at Burrs, sees 'Canadian Pacific' passing with a demonstration freight. High on Holcombe Hill in the background is the 128-feet-high Peel Tower built in 1852 to commemorate Sir Robert Peel (1788-1850) a local politician who as Home Secretary set up the Metropolitan Police in London which proved to be the starting point for the national police force. (The nickname 'Bobbies' originated from his Christian name.)

Set against a dark background the low afternoon sun glints off the locomotive, and picks out the stock of another freight train working its way south.

The River Irwell is crossed for the last time on the return trip with the first colours of autumn appearing on the tips of the trees.

Mid-winter reveals much more of the bridge, and the locomotive exhaust hanging in the cold air above the carriages.

In October 2003, on the eve of an enthusiast's weekend, a night photography event was staged at Bury Bolton Street Station with locomotives positioned in the platforms giving the impression of night-time arrivals and departures.

Opposite: Arrival back at Bury on a cold December morning. Only the footprints of this hardy photographer have disturbed the carpet of newly fallen snow this far down the platform.

I couldn't resist framing the locomotive within the station name board, but believe me it took some time to get the composition right.

At the time work on the signal gantry was still in progress, but the arms and lights were temporarily positioned on their posts for the benefit of the photographers.

Up until 6 September 2003 our journey would have terminated here. However, on that day, following years of hard work involving the reinstatement of demolished bridges and construction of new ones, the 4-mile extension to Heywood opened to complete a 12-mile preserved railway enjoyed by thousands of visitors every year.

Opposite: With Bury in the distance this '1940s Wartime Weekend' train has just crossed the M66 motorway on its way to the new station at Heywood.

This photograph, taken long before the Society was able to run passenger trains, shows the derelict state of all that remained at Heywood Station and serves to illustrate the amount of work that was necessary before re-opening could be considered.

As ever the volunteers were up to the task and the whole station area has been transformed to provide all necessary facilities for the travelling public.

From the platform there's a panoramic view across a typical Lancashire mill-town landscape with the Pennines providing a spectacular, snow-capped, backdrop.

The extensive cobbled car park provides an ideal location for other societies to hold rallies. On this occasion visitors were able to combine a trip behind an historic steam locomotive with a chance to view a collection of Morris Minors assembled to celebrate a classic piece of motoring history.

One of the objectives of re-opening the Heywood line was to retain a direct link with the national rail network which would not only allow visiting main line certified locomotives to arrive by rail but would also provide future opportunities for excursions to and from the railway. The two locomotives being hauled back to Bury in this picture had actually returned from an event at Manchester's Victoria Station.

Opposite: When the Heywood link was re-opened the East Lancashire Railway became the first, and so far only, preserved line to cross over a motorway, which has no doubt surprised a considerable number of people travelling along the M66!

Approaching the outskirts of Bury the train is passing over Seven Arches Viaduct which carries the line over the River Roche. At this point the river forms the natural boundary between Heywood and Bury. The locomotive is former London Midland and Scottish Railway 4-6-2 Princess Royal Class No. 6201 'Princess Elizabeth' named after Her Majesty. Peel Tower stands high on Holcombe Hill in the distance.

The journey is complete as the train from Heywood pulls in alongside platform 2.

However, on special event weekends, the locomotive works at Buckley Wells are open to the public and a shuttle service operates from platform 4.

The short journey is often in the hands of a visiting industrial tank engine. In 1998, as part of its centenary celebrations, the former Manchester Ship Canal Company locomotive No. 14 'St Johns' was brought in to perform these duties. Normally based on the Severn Valley Railway it has spent much of its preservation life in the red livery it had carried working for its second owners, the Dyestuffs Division of ICI at Blackley in Manchester, where it had been given the name 'The Lady Armaghdale'. The original black livery, carried here, had been applied at Bury for the centenary events. On its return to the Severn Valley it was returned to the guise of Thomas the Tank Engine and continued to entertain children of all ages at preserved railways up and down the country.

A regular visitor to work the shuttles travels across the Pennines from the Keighley and Worth Valley Railway. Former Lancashire & Yorkshire 0-4-0 Saddletank No. 51218 is one of only two survivors from no fewer than fifty-seven tiny locomotives built for the Lancashire and Yorkshire Railway between 1891 and 1910. They were initially intended to shunt the dock lines at Fleetwood, Goole and Liverpool and quickly became known as 'Pugs'. The name has stuck with them into preservation.

The shed's Locomotive Arrangement Board provides all necessary information on the status of all the locomotives currently based on the railway, be they in traffic or under overhaul.

In August 1993 the railway's locomotive department relocated from Castlecroft to the former ex-British Rail Electric Car shop at Buckley Wells. This building has had a variety of uses through its lifetime including operating as both an electric and diesel multiple unit depot. It has now been returned to its original East Lancashire Railway use as a well equipped steam locomotive shed and workshop.

In superb lighting at dusk the National Railway Museum's 'Duchess of Hamilton' simmers on shed at the end of a day's work.

A reminder that the 'bread and butter' purpose for the shed's existence is the maintenance, repair and overhaul of the railway's fleet of locomotives.

Opposite: But it is a great place to photograph steam at night and special evenings, for that very purpose, are often arranged during enthusiast weekends.

The beauty of these evenings is that you are able to experiment with a variety of portraits which do not have to include the whole locomotive in the frame to create an atmospheric image.

Opposite: Artificial floodlighting picks out the detail of the former Southern Railway's Class S15 4-6-0 locomotive No. 30506, a visitor from the Mid Hants Railway. Natural moonlight provides interest in the night sky.

Two giants of steam from original rival railway companies stand side by side under the Buckley Wells lights. This photograph was carefully composed to ensure that the same length of each locomotive was visible in the frame.

Three giants from the diesel age captured under similar circumstances. This class, known as 'Deltics', was introduced to replace the express steam locomotives that operated on the East Coast main line between London and Edinburgh.

The original 48278 was withdrawn from Rosegrove shed, Burnley, at the very end of British Railways' steam on 3 August 1968. The final working was as the Copy Pit Banker, used to assist heavy trains climbing Copy Pit from Todmorden by pushing from the rear. For its last duties the loco had been chalked with inscriptions to mark that final day. The finale of the ELR's 'Festival of Steam' in 1993 was the recreation of that final working with the visiting, Keighley and Worth Valley Railway's, No 48431 suitably decorated. A reunion of former Rosegrove firemen and drivers also took place. This photograph, taken on the eve of the festival's final day serves as a reminder that, but for the dedication of railway preservationists, 1968 would indeed have been the end of steam.